THIS JOURNAL
BELONGS TO

_____

I DON'T EAT ANYTHING THAT FARTS

One to change
a few A few to
change many
Many to change
the world
Starts with one

Life Is Too Short To Make Others Shorter

Animals are
not products

Life doesn't
have a price

The only animals I eat are crackers

Please don't refuse with your eyes what the animals endure with their bodies

If you can
be anything,
Be kind

Thank you for purchasing our Journal
We hope you like it, If you did, would you consider posting a review online?
This helps us to continue providing great products, and helps potential buyers make confident decisions.

Thank you in advance for your review and for being a favorite!

Younistic Word Publishing

Manufactured by Amazon.ca
Bolton, ON